Is there anything there at the top of the stair?

Poems About Being Scared

By **Brian Moses**

With illustrations
by **Mike Gordon**

HODDER
Wayland

An imprint of Hodder Children's Books

Text copyright © Brian Moses 2000

Editor: Sarah Doughty
Designer: Sarah Massini

Published in 2000 by
Hodder Wayland, an imprint of
Hodder Children's Books

A Cataloguing record for this book is available
from the British Library

ISBN 0 7502 2798 2

Printed and bound in Hong Kong by Wing King Tong

Hodder Children's Books
A division of Hodder Headline Ltd
338 Euston Road, London NW1 3BH

**Most of the illustrations in this book
were first used in the title
I Feel Frightened by Brian Moses
(Hodder Wayland, 1994).**

Contents

At the top of the stairs

What will I find
at the top of the stairs?
Do the shadows hide ghosts
or fierce grizzly bears?

Will something nasty
jump out at me?
Will it leave me trembling
helplessly?

I'd much rather somebody
took my hand
and led me upstairs
to that shadowy land.

Spider under my bed

I'm not frightened of
mice or rats,
earwigs, slugs,
beetles or bats.
Dark shadows or ghosts
don't fill me with dread,
but I'm really scared of
a
spider –
under
my
bed.

Put your hands up
and come on out –
I always know
when you're about.

A funny feeling
spreads over me,
you're down there, I know,
even though I can't see.

So put your hands up
and come on out,
this time I'm brave,
I'm not going to shout... **AAARGH**!

Put your hands up

7

Scary books

I hate it when my brother
reads his scary books.
He reads them out loud
and gives me nasty looks.

He says there's a ghost
in our room at night,
he makes ghostly noises
and gives me a fright.

I dream bad dreams
about vampires and spooks,
I hate it when my brother
reads his scary books.

9

Under the covers

Don't be so silly,
I try to tell myself.
It isn't a horrible hairy hand
that's sitting on my shelf.

It isn't a sleeping vampire bat
on the hook behind my door,
but I'd best dive under the covers
because I'm not absolutely sure!

Things that go bump...

Things that go bump in the night
often give me a terrible fright.
I can feel my heart jump
when something goes bump,

I can feel myself shake
as I'm lying awake,
and with every little noise I hear
I imagine that something awful will appear.

11

When I'm scared

A quivering jelly on a plate,

that's me,

when I'm scared.

A mouse in need of a Supermate,

that's me,

when I'm scared.

Little Miss Muffet
finding a spider
has dropped in for tea
and landed beside her...

That's me,
can't you see,
I'm all these things
when I'm scared!

A silly song

If I sing a silly song,

it's not that I want to annoy you.

It's not that I want you

to sing along.

It's just that I'm scared

and it helps if I sing

my silly song.

Let's pretend…

I'm a fearless superhero,
scared of no one, nothing, zero!

If you're frightened, call for me,
I'm brave and daring as you will see.
Nothing makes me run away,

I can sort out the bad guys any day
for I'm a fearless superhero,
scared of no one, nothing, zero!

Dad hates rollercoasters

My Dad hates riding on rollercoasters,
they really make his face turn pale.
He's terrified of the downhill ride,
he thinks the brakes will fail.

And although I'm scared of lots of things
I get a terrific thrill
from riding a rollercoaster,
but Dad says they make him feel ill!

Mum hates flying

Mum says she's frightened of flying,
she'd rather keep her feet on the ground.
She doesn't like taking off
and she doesn't like coming down.

She won't look out the window,
she sits with her eyes shut tight.
The very worst thing for Mum
is when she has to go on a flight.

Please don't make me jump,
I just don't like it one bit.
It's easy to make me tremble
and give me a shivering fit.

Don't sound a loud noise behind me
or jump out at me and say '**BOO**!'
You know that I really don't like it,
but I like to do it to you!

My trick on Grandma

I shouldn't have done it I know,

it upset Grandma a lot,

she had to sit down in her chair,

it made her go cold and then hot.

She's always kind to me

and now I feel very sad,

my spider-in-a-box-trick

made Grandma feel really bad.

19

On my first day at school
I wished I'd stayed home.
On my first day at school
I hated being alone.

at school

But my teacher was kind
and I soon made a friend.
When Mum called at 3 o'clock
I didn't want the day to end.

The storm

My teddy hates a storm
when the thunder rumbles close by.
He hates it when the lightning flashes
and zigzags part the sky.

So we hide beneath the table
with my fingers in teddy's ears.
In a storm he depends on me
to be brave and calm his fears.

Goodnight poem

As I grow older

I'm sure to get bolder.

Then most of my fears

should disappear…

Hooray!

Index of first lines

About Brian Moses

Brian Moses is really a Superhero although he doesn't tell many people! When he's not out righting wrongs, he can be found

in St. Leonards-on-Sea with his wife Anne (a Superheroine), their daughters, Karen and Linette, two overweight guinea pigs, three nervous fish and a tame squirrel. When he isn't writing at home, Brian travels round reading his poems in schools, libraries, bookshops and at festivals. He plays a variety of percussion instruments to underpin the rhythm. You might like some of his other poetry books, published by Hodder Wayland.